The Simplification of Becoming a Millionaire

GARY L. CLARK

Strategic Book Publishing and Rights Co.

Strategic Book Publishing and Rights Co.
12620 FM 1960, Suite A4-507
Houston, TX 77065
www.sbpra.com

ISBN: 978-1-62516-854-2

Interior Book Design: Judy Maenle

Acknowledgements

I want to express my appreciation and love to my wife for her caring, loving patience and support on the journey we have traveled over the years.

I also want to express my appreciation to Doris Bloodsworth who shared her time and knowledge.

I especially want to thank the clients that had the confidence and trust in me to allow me to be their financial partner.

In addition, I want to thank the U.S. Navy, Sears, Wal-Mart and Ameriprise Financial for giving me the opportunities to learn, grow, and help others through the wonderful journey of this great life I have had and continue to have.

The Simplification of Becoming a Millionaire

Introduction   vii

CHAPTER 1   Background Story   1

CHAPTER 2   Brief History of the Stock Market   6

CHAPTER 3   Getting Started   10

CHAPTER 4   Mentality for Investing   14

CHAPTER 5   Financial Life   17

CHAPTER 6   How to Invest   22

CHAPTER 7   Types of Investments   26

CHAPTER 8   Asset Allocation   31

Conclusion   36

Epilogue   39

About the Author   41

Introduction

The primary purpose for writing this book is not for it to be a "Do It Yourself" Guide, but to encourage you to begin taking steps that will help you to accumulate wealth and enhance your financial life.

Most importantly, it is to point out how easy it is to become a millionaire just by taking a few simple steps. Remember, it is not about luck, it is about you taking the right steps with the right advisor and the discipline to stay focused, pay yourself selfishly and enjoying the ride along the way.

CHAPTER 1

Background Story

There is a phrase that I'm sure you have heard, "if I can do it, anyone can." To understand the simplifications of it all, I think that it is important to know my story.

I was born in a small country town called Summerfield, in North Carolina. I grew up in a family that was very poor. There were five boys, and my mother, who was divorced, often worked two jobs cleaning homes for others. We were often taken care of by my grandmother. We lived in a house that had two rooms. Our mother and grandmother slept in one room and all the boys slept in the other. During the day, our one room served as a kitchen, etcetera.

There were many occasions where we would have to steal apples and chickens to eat. Shoes with cardboard cutouts for soles and jeans that were patched in many places were considered a luxury. We did not have electricity nor indoor plumbing and only a "one seater" outside for a bathroom.

Since I was the oldest son, it was my responsibility to take care of my brothers. Little did I realize that this would help me to mature early. Later, at age fifteen, I was told by a young girl I liked that I "acted too old." To me, this was a compliment.

There were many mornings when I had to make fires in an old cast iron wood stove, getting up very early to make sure that it was warm when the rest of the family would get up. Often, I would be the last one to bed and the first to get up after four hours of sleep.

I began working at age six in a garage for a man that allowed me to sweep floors, wash parts for cars, and anything else that needed to be done. My pay was about two dollars a week, I learned the importance of working hard and it kept me out of trouble. Also, I was fortunate enough to work with a gentleman who later became one of the largest figures in NASCAR, Richard Childress.

While working at the garage, the owner's son began building a race car for two brothers. They would work on the car all week, race in Winston-Salem on Saturday night, tear the car up and do it again. Little did I know that these young men, who I used to laugh at, would become world-famous entrepreneurs.

Going to school gave me the opportunity to meet others and exposed me to the world of learning. For some reason, I really enjoyed reading. On one occasion, I read so much that I temporarily went blind. This was caused by poor lighting from the use of kerosene lamps to see by. Nonetheless, reading opened up a world that I had never known.

Unfortunately, learning came so easy, that I became bored. At one point I was told that I was the smartest in my class. According to a counselor, I was so smart that I should learn to become a cook. During this period, schools were segregated and minorities could only do certain types of jobs.

The garage that I was working at later was bought by a small trucking company which I began working for. The world of trucking is a story in itself. I will shorten the story by saying this: the world of trucking exposed me to a whole different way of life. This allowed me to begin to travel. Prior to this time, I'd never been any farther than twenty miles from Summerfield, North Carolina. I found that I enjoyed going different places and meeting different people.

Unfortunately, when I graduated from high school the Vietnam War was at its peak. Eventually, two of my brothers and I were drafted. At one point my two brothers were in Vietnam in full combat. It had to be torture for my mother.

During this period just about everyone knew someone in the military that had been shot, disabled or killed. A cousin had both legs blown off. I made a decision, that rather than be drafted in the Army, I would join the Navy. Again, this decision turns out to be a good one. I was exposed to a lot of different people, able to visit a lot of different countries and most importantly, being in the military helped instill discipline, responsibility, and respect for others.

The most important aspect of the military was that it allowed me to go to college on the G.I. Bill. Prior to going into the military, I never contemplated ever going to college. Why? Simply because there was no money to do so. The thought was to graduate from high school, get married, have a family, work somewhere for forty years and retire.

While in the Navy, there was a young officer who tried to impress his girlfriend by coming over to myself and two buddies while we were walking back to the barracks, on the other side of the street, and yelling, "Hey sailor don't you know to salute an officer?"

We looked at him, smiled, saluted, and once he was gone, began laughing. This was a very important event in my life.

At that very moment, I said to myself and my buddies, "if all it takes to be a salutor or salutee is a four-year degree, I can do that." I decided then and there to go to college.

When I got out of the military, I moved back to Greensboro, North Carolina, and began loading trucks at Sears. At that time if you were drafted in the military, companies were required to take you back and reinstate your job. I appreciate Sears to this day.

After I got back to Greensboro and was back at work, I began going to school at Guilford College. By the time I finished two and a half years later, we had a wonderful daughter (Tracy), and a wonderful son (Lee). While in school, I was working approximately forty to forty-five hours a week loading trucks, carrying eighteen to twenty-three hours per quarter in school, and helping to raise our family. To this day I have no tolerance for people who say they don't have time to do things.

The military, marriage, and college were pivotal moments in my life because it again further instilled the importance of discipline and responsibility.

When I finished Guilford, rather than pursue law school, I went to work for Sears in their human resource department. One of my primary responsibilities was to represent employees. While 401(k) plans are common now, very few companies were using them at that time.

Because very few people knew anything about the stock market, I would get a lot of questions regarding investing. Because of the position that I was in, it was very important for me to be knowledgeable about the markets, investing, and risk associated with it all.

Between my position and later becoming involved in an investment club with two friends (William James and

Leroy Bethea), I became very knowledgeable about the basics of the markets and investing, and more importantly, it was something I enjoyed.

After twenty years with Sears, I left the company to start my own business. After several successful businesses, I decided to do something I enjoyed doing: helping people and giving financial advice. After interviewing with several firms, I decided to go work for the firm that is today the largest financial planning company, Amerprise Financial Services. By the time I retired I had earned several awards, which included financial advisor of the year, and was recognized with a 100 percent client satisfaction award. During the fifteen years that I worked as a financial advisor many of my clients became financially comfortable, and are today enjoying comfortable retirements.

This book demonstrates how taking a few simple steps can possibly help you move toward becoming a millionaire as well.

CHAPTER 2

Brief History of the Stock Market

According to Robert Stammers CFA (Investopedia), a semblance of a stock exchange started as far back as 1531 in Antwerp. Brokers and moneylenders would meet there to deal in business, government, and individual debt issues. While there were no shares traded, there were many flavors of business and financier partnerships that produced instruments like stocks.

He further states that in the sixteen hundreds, the Dutch, British, and French governments all gave charters to companies within the West Indies in their names. On the cusp of imperialism's high point it seemed like everyone had a stake in the profits from the East Indies and Asia, except the people living there and the sea voyagers that bought back goods from the East. These travels were very risky. On top of the Barbary Pirates, there were risks of weather and poor navigation.

In order to lessen the risk of loss, ship owners had long been in the practice of seeking investors who would put up money for the voyage, outfitting the ship and crew. In return they would receive a percentage of the proceeds if the voyage was successful. These early limited liability companies lasted for only a single voyage. Investors spread their risk by investing in several different ventures at the same time. They would be playing the odds against all of them, ending in disaster.

These East India companies changed the way business was being done. These companies had stocks that would pay dividends on all of the proceeds from all of the voyages the companies would take. These were the first modern joint stock companies. This allowed the companies to demand more for their shares and build larger fleets.

Because the shares in the various East India companies were issued on paper, investors could sell the papers to other investors. Because there was no stock exchange, the investor would have to track down a broker to carry out a trade.

In England, most brokers and investors did their business in various coffee shops around town. Debt issues and shares were written up and posted on doors or mailed as newsletters. The British East India Company had one of the biggest competitive advantages and financial history, a government-backed monopoly. When investors began to receive huge dividends and sell their shares for fortunes, other investors were hungry for a piece of the action. The budding financial boom in England came so quickly that there were no rules and regulations for the issuing of shares.

The South Seas Company emerged with a similar charter from the King. Its shares and the numerous reissues sold as soon as they were listed. Before the first ship ever left the harbor, the South Seas Company had used its newfound investor fortune to open posh offices in the best parts of London.

Because of their success, the businessmen rushed in to offer new shares in their own ventures. Some were as ludicrous as reclaiming sunshine from vegetables or better yet, a company promising investor shares in an undertaking of such vast importance that they can't be revealed. All the shares sold.

Eventually, the markets crashed and the government outlawed the issuing of shares until 1825.

In the United States, the Philadelphia Stock exchange was one of the first markets in the US. However the New York Stock Exchange, which began in 1792, became the most powerful.

The New York Stock Exchange was formed by a few brokers under a Buttonwood tree and made its home on Wall Street. It was at the heart of all business, with trade coming and going to and from the US, as well as the domestic base for most banks and large corporations. By setting listings requirements and amending fees, the NYSE became a very wealthy institution.

As time passed, the NYSE grew as America grew. As its international prestige grew, it soon became the most important stock exchange in the world.

Contrary to what most people believe, the stock market will go up more than it will go down. Over the past hundred years, while the market has gone up and down, it is important to remember that the Dow Jones in 1912–13 was at 88.42. It wasn't until November 1972 that it broke 1,000 points. The high for the market in October 2007, when it closed at over 14,000.

The lowest point since the 14,000 mark was when it dropped to 6,600 points in March of 2009. At the time of this writing (May, 2013), the market is back over 15,000 points, four years after the Great Recession. The important points to remember here are, the market has come a long way in the past hundred years, and that it has constantly moved up and down. *A lot more up than down.*

Over the past hundred years, certainly there have been crashes, some worse than others. However, they all pass, and the down markets become opportunities to buy. As I would say to my clients, "a down market is your friend."

According to Fredric S. Mishkin and Eugene White in their paper "U.S. Stock Market Crashes and their Aftermath: Implications for Monetary Policy," a crash is defined by a market dropping 20 percent or more.

In most American minds, there are three major crashes that have occurred which can be called dramatic: the 1929 crash, the crash of 1987, and the most recent crash in October of 2007 to March 2009. During that period, the market dropped from 14,164.53 to 6,626.94. This was a drop of approximately 7,538 points. While the averages have been somewhat dramatic over a period of time, some days or weeks have been very dramatic.

Again, according to Mushkin and White, from July 1919 to August 1921, the market dropped 41.2 percent. From April 1930 to May 1932, the market dropped 81.8 percent. Since their paper was written, during the crash of 2007 to 2009 the market dropped nearly 47 percent.

While dramatic crashes have occurred and probably always will, it is important to remember that the "dramatic events" are only temporary. They can occur for many reasons, because of poor monetary policy, world events, 9/11s, assassinations, etcetera, but it is more important to stay focused on your financial goals and keep the emotions out of your financial life.

CHAPTER 3

Getting Started

The simplification of becoming a millionaire is, as stated, "simple." It is very important to develop (1) a mindset that you want to do this and (2) the discipline to do so.

While an advisor, it always amazed me how willing people were to pay someone else, or to pay for something else, rather than pay themselves. While the concept of paying oneself is not new, for some reason, most people do not buy into the concept. As I often told clients, if they are not "paying themselves," they are getting up every day, going to work for someone else.

Think about this: no matter what your income is, if you don't save or invest any of your money for yourself, then 100 percent of what you earn is being paid out to everyone or something else. It does not matter if it is going toward rent or mortgage, food, automobiles, pets, groceries, or taxes, you are not receiving anything for the person that is working hardest for the income.

So, to get started, begin today by putting in place steps to start to pay yourself first. Not doing so is unacceptable. Now, to be clear, to pay yourself first, before any of your money goes to anyone else, put in place a system that allows you to automatically begin doing so. While there are many books on different strategies, I often recommended my clients read *The Automatic Millionaire* by David Beck. I found it to be an easy and understandable read.

There are several ways to have money taken out of your check automatically. Some companies have systems in place whereby you can have certain amounts sent to a specific institution, such as a bank, investment firms, or individuals. One of the simplest ways to "pay yourself," is via a company retirement account. For all of you who think you can't afford to save anything, the fact is, you can't afford not to. For example, if you are not saving into a retirement plan that is tax-deductible, which reduces your "taxable" income and thereby possibly reducing your taxes, then you are happily paying good old Uncle Sam. For example, if your median income is $1,200 weekly, and you don't save into a retirement plan, all of it is taxed. However, if you begin paying yourself $200 weekly, your taxable income drops to $1,000 weekly. So rather than the money going to your favorite uncle (Sam), your taxes on that income are reduced.

If you are thirty-five years of age, work another thirty years and do this, not only will you reduce your taxable income by $10,400 annually, but you also have the potential to grow those dollars to $312,000 over that time frame. If you invest this money for the period, at a 9 percent rate of return, you will have the potential to grow those dollars to approximately $1,500,000.

There are several ways to get started. One, you can do it yourself. However, most people don't have the knowledge or time to do so. Two, hire a financial advisor. Some people feel they can't afford a financial advisor. I say again, you can't afford not to. You don't know what you don't know.

In 1986 when I first went into business, I had an accountant to help me to set up the different tax schedules, etcetera. I paid my taxes, Social Security, and other appropriate expenses on a monthly basis. At the end of the year, I was given an enormous tax bill. I asked the accountant why the taxes owed were so high, especially since I had been paying throughout the year. He was not as emotional about it as I was (he didn't have to pay it). He simply said, "It is what it is, you need to pay."

I then asked how I could avoid having to pay as much tax the following year. He told me that I needed to get a financial advisor and could use more write-offs. During this time, financial advisors were not as common as in today's environment. I asked what the advisor could do for me. Unfortunately, he could not tell me. So I told him, "You take care of the taxes, I'll take care of the write-offs and investing." During this time, I thought that the only thing advisors could do was invest your money.

Because he could not tell me the advantages of having an advisor, instead of "paying myself," I found creative ways to have write-offs and other ways to reduce my tax liability. By doing so, and not knowing what I didn't know, I paid a lot of other people money that could have been paid to me and my family.

What I later found out when I became a financial advisor was there are many strategies that a person or small business owner can take that not only would allow one to reduce their tax liability, but accumulate wealth as well. The bottom line is, had I begun using a financial advisor in 1987, I would have accumulated far more wealth than I did.

To summarize how to get started:

1. Commit to begin "paying yourself."
2. Find ways to "do it now."
3. Set up "automatic systems" to do so.
4. Find a financial partner (financial advisor) to work with.

If you are young and begin saving as little as $50 weekly, investing in a "moderately aggressive to aggressive" portfolio earning an annual rate of return of 9 to 10 percent, by the time you retire you can have over $1,000,000. Obviously, if you are older, the more you will need to save, but this is what an advisor can tell you.

CHAPTER 4

Mentality for Investing

I began investing when I was about twenty-four years of age. At the time I did not have a clue. I remember reading about Warren Buffet and how he had become wealthy by investing in this thing called the stock market. At the time, Berkshire Hathaway's stock was selling for a little over $300 per share. Needless to say, the cost per share was a lot more than we could afford to pay for at the time. However, the lesson learned was that one could invest, stay invested and accumulate wealth. Also, reading about Mr. Buffett's philosophy, I learned that when the market was bad, that could be a good thing. Buying undervalued stock allowed you to accumulate a lot more shares.

To begin investing, I will repeat what I said in the previous chapter. Get a "Financial Partner" that can help you to make informed and unemotional decisions. The most important point I want to make in this chapter is to develop a mentality that allows you not to make decisions based on "fear or greed." While some think that the "buy and hold" philosophy is no longer good strategy, I would say they are wrong. What may not be a good strategy is buying and selling individual stocks when you can only afford to get a few shares.

In today's market environment, it is hard to be an investor who relies on getting wealthy by individual stock selection. Unless you can afford to buy thousands of shares and develop your own portfolio with diversity, you are taking extreme risk. For most people the research, monitoring, and resources are not available. Unless you have $100,000 to set up your own stock portfolio, consider Exchange Traded Funds (ETFs) or mutual funds. They allow you to invest in multiple companies with expert management, and a diverse portfolio while minimizing risk.

As I indicated earlier, develop a non-emotional, long term investment approach. Maintain the mentality that a down market is your best friend. In a down market, three things happen:

1. If you are systematically investing, the average cost per share will go down every time additional shares are purchased at the lower price.
2. By investing and continuing to invest in a down market, you are able to accumulate many more shares.
3. When the market turns around (and it will), you will achieve a higher rate of return not only on your newly bought investments, but your older investments as well.

The bottom line is, develop and maintain a "have no fear," non-emotional, long-term, and "down market is my best friend" mentality. It will work. There are no get rich quick solutions. Many people have tried the "get rich quick" approach and have ended up on the losing end.

Above all, "pay yourself" until it hurts. Think "investing" rather than just saving money. With an investing mentality, your money is more apt to grow at a higher rate of

Gary L. Clark

return than your savings rate. The question you should ask yourself, *Would I rather have an average rate of return of 10 percent or 1.5 percent?* This is called a no-brainer.

CHAPTER 5

Financial Life

One of the most important points in helping to understand how to accumulate wealth is to understand the importance of your "financial life." It is my belief that one's financial life is as important, if not more important, than one's personal life.

This may seem like a strange thing to say, however, there are very few things worse than growing old without the financial wherewithal to live comfortably for your whole life.

When I talk of your financial life, I am talking about the different financial stages that you go through from the time of birth to death. Every phase is crucial. It is important that one learns about finances when young. This can and will set the tone for the rest of your financial life. It is essential that parents teach their children about finance, investing, and financial planning for the future.

Today, the financial environment is different from the time that your parents or grandparents grew up. While there has always been risk and uncertainty in financial lives, there were not as many factors that created "dramatic moments" in planning and investing. The most important thing to remember, even in today's environment, is to always know where you want to go financially and stay focused on each phase of your financial life.

As indicated earlier, there are several stages to a financial life and many things can happen during these stages. Again, in today's environment, one is more apt to lose a job, have medical issues not covered, a spouse lose their job, a teenager creating issues, and just plain life where stuff happens. Through all of these things, it is important to put things in place to make sure that disruptions do not change your main goal. This goal is to accumulate enough wealth to have and maintain a comfortable life.

One theme that I am constantly emphasizing is do not be afraid to use a financial advisor. Again, you don't know what you don't know, and it does not hurt to have a financial partner (advisor) to help you through all the phases of your financial life.

Another important point to remember is that each disruption will possibly create unnecessary change in your financial life. What direction you take will be very important, and having someone that will give you options is necessary to stay focused.

As you move through the financial phases, you'll want to avoid as many financial killers as possible. One of the worst "killers" is credit card debt. Credit cards are like fire: if used properly, they can be very helpful in getting the things you need to enhance your life. But if used the wrong way, they can burn you badly.

Another financial killer is living beyond your means. You are where you are only at this moment. When it comes to having more or living a different lifestyle, you can work to earn more money via promotions, moves, etcetera, or put yourself in a different position through additional education, technical or higher degrees. A point to remember is to learn to always live within your means.

While there are many financial killers, one of the most dramatic is the selection of your life partner. While love is important, it is just as important to know what the other person is bringing to the table. You want to make sure that your partner is focused on the same goals, has the same level of maturity, is responsible, and is willing to do what needs to be done to help enjoy life through every financial phase, as well as to make any necessary adjustments along the way.

From a financial planning standpoint, there are six basic steps you should consider. The first step is to know where you are now. This is like a financial x-ray. What do you have, what are you doing, and what steps are being taken to move forward?

The second step is to understand where you are from a protection standpoint. Do you have disability and life protection? Most people will have some type of coverage with their employers. However, if you lose your job, coverage will more than likely go away. One of the main reasons that families go bankrupt is due to disability or death. You want to make sure that you have enough disability and life insurance to take care of yourself, your family, and those you may leave behind. If you are not sure how much life insurance coverage you need, check with your financial advisor.

A simple concept to use is the "DIME" concept. This concept includes the sum of Debt, Income, Mortgage and Education. For example, if debt owed is $20,000, the mortgage is $250,000, income is $50,000 annually, and your education goal is $200,000, you have an approximate need of $520,000 of coverage. Keep in mind that this is a minimum that you should have.

Once you get older, you will want to consider "Long Term Care." The purpose of this protection is to cover nursing care when you are old and do not want your family to take care of you. Do not impose this burden on anyone. This is another area where most families will experience bankruptcy.

The third step is to know what your risk level is, as well as your time frame. The level of risk you are willing to take and the level you need to take may be two different things. Understanding your time frame as to how long you have to get where you want to go and/or how long will it take to get there is very important. Prior to investing money, make sure that you have at least two months income in a savings account.

Fourth, develop tax strategies that will prevent the "tax tail" from wagging the "tax dog." Know what strategies are needed to affect taxes now and what steps are put in place that will help in the future as well.

The fifth step is to answer the question, "When do I want to retire?" Set a time frame and the amount that you will need to live on for the rest of your life. It is important to plan for the long term. People are living much longer than before. If you are married, there is a very strong chance that you or your partner may live to age ninety-two. If you take care of yourself, it may be possible to live even longer.

Lastly, make sure that you put an estate plan in place. In other words, have wills, trusts (if necessary), living wills, powers of attorney, and a health surrogate named to make sure that your wishes are carried out the way you want and not like someone else wants. More importantly, make your passing as stress-free as possible for your family.

CHAPTER 6

Investing

Investing can mean many things to many people. However, for the purpose of this book, I am talking about investing in the stock market. As I indicated before, investing in the stock market offers greater potential for the accumulation and appreciation of your financial assets than almost any other type of investments.

In regards to investing, don't try to guess when there is a good time or when there is a right time to get into the markets. History has shown that moving in and out of the market will cost you time and money. As mentioned earlier, simply being out of the market can cause missing "upsides" in the market or worse, missing out on buying more shares at a lower price when the market is down.

When you buy more shares at a lower price, it reduces your overall cost per share. As I often like to say, "a down market is your best friend." The reason is because a down market allows you to accumulate more shares at a lower price, reduce overall cost per share, and generate more dividends in the long run.

Needless to say, in volatile markets, if you get caught up in the emotion of it all, it can be trying. The key is to not get emotional. This is a good point at which to remind you of the importance of a good advisor who will move you through these periods with sound advice. The key is to stay fully invested with a diversified portfolio.

Some of the things to be considered when investing are: risk tolerance, time frame, objectives, and asset allocations based on the aforementioned.

Your risk tolerance and whether you should have a conservative, moderate conservative, moderate, moderate aggressive, or aggressive posture should also depend on your time frame.

Risk tolerance – based on the definition of risk, "the probability for loss." In other words, how much of a risk are you willing to take not to lose your money or as I like to say, *grow your money*. After being involved in investing since the early seventies, I have learned, if there is a strategic plan with the appropriate asset allocation, you have very little risk that is being taken. In other words, you have "controlled risk."

Since the early seventies, the stock market has appreciated from approximately 1,000 points to over 15,000 points as of March 2013. As a general rule, the market will go up a little, over six and a half to seven years, out of every ten years. That means it goes down a little over three out of every ten years. In other words, you have twice as much chance of your assets appreciating as you so do of losing them. The point is you should take the "have no fear" attitude when investing. There will always be dramatic events, but those events will pass. Investing without risk is about time and discipline, and as I have said earlier, you do this by making investing a non-emotional event. In other words, if you are young and just starting, with the exception of "cash reserves," or emergency money, you may want to consider an aggressive posture. Because of your time frame, you have a lot of time to make up for corrections in the market. However, if you are close to retirement (55–65), you may want to consider a risk tolerance of moderate aggressive to moderate. Now, if you have not accumulated enough assets needed for retirement, you may want to take a more aggressive posture, extend your time frame for growing assets and prolong your retirement date. In considering your risk tolerance, you should consider appropriate rates of return.

Conservative – cash, Certificates of Deposit (CDs), money markets – 3%

Moderate conservative – stocks: 30%; bonds: 70% – 4 to 7%

Moderate – bonds: 50%; stocks: 50% – 6.5–8%

Moderate aggressive – bonds: 35%; stocks: 65% – 8 to 10%

Aggressive – stocks: 100% – 10 to 14%

While these are approximate rates of return, the time you stay invested, systematic investing and reinvested dividends, will have an impact on your actual returns. I cannot overemphasize the importance of staying invested. Simply missing a few days over time can mean a modest return rather than a very good return. For example, after the financial debacle of 2008 many investors, out of fear, not only got out of the market, but were afraid to get back in. In March 2009, the market was at a low of approximately 6,600 points. As of today, it stands over 15,000 points. That's over 100 percent return in four years.

One mistake a lot of retirees make, is to get too conservative, and they will get completely out of the market and go into cash or CDs. What has happened over the past few years is that these types of vehicles, when you take inflation and the overall cost of living into account, have actually lost money, especially their purchasing power. The reason to stay invested is to continue to grow your assets, to outpace inflation and the cost of living. Remember, investing is about time and not about timing.

In addition to staying invested in a moderate conservative to moderate portfolio if retired, also consider continuing systematically investing a portion of your discretionary dollars into the market. It is a lot better trying to decide how you're going to pass assets to your heirs than trying to figure out how you're going to make it. In other words, you can never have too much money.

By the way, being able to give is a good thing.

Understanding these steps and knowing how to achieve the steps is an important reason to have a good financial partner (advisor).

CHAPTER 7

Types of Investments

In today's environment there are many types of vehicles to invest in. You have Annuities, ETFs, Options, Mutual Funds, and Life Insurance, just to name a few.

It's important to remember when setting up a portfolio, to be well diversified. Again, as mentioned in the previous chapter, based on your time frame and risk tolerance, your portfolio should reflect the appropriate mix of the different types of investment vehicles. A good financial advisor can determine the appropriate mix.

There are many fund families that will offer "turnkey" portfolios that will have a variety of investments inside of the funds themselves. Based on the level of management of the particular vehicle, the fund manager may have a "hands-on" approach or set up a portfolio and rebalance over certain periods of time, such as monthly or quarterly. Obviously, the fee based products should be more hands-on and be structured in a way to reduce volatility as well as generate a good return.

When I talk about types of investments, the basic ones are cash, bonds, individual stocks, mutual funds, annuities, and life insurance. Each has its advantages and disadvantages.

Cash – what you see is what you get. In today's environment, interest paid on cash is at an all-time low. You will earn very little, if any return. While most think money is safe, with no return, you are losing money. Again, while inflation may be low, your purchasing power is reduced because your dollars are worth less each year. It is also possible to be taxed on interest that is earned. Cash vehicles include checking accounts, savings accounts, CDs, and money market funds.

Bonds – a bond by definition is a fixed financial interest paying asset issued by governments, companies, banks, utility companies, or other entities. The issuer agrees to pay the investor a certain percent of interest over a certain period of time.

There are many types of bonds. Like stocks, you can have a conservative portfolio, US government-backed bonds for example, to an aggressive portfolio of high yield bonds. These can include corporate bonds to junk bonds.

The advantage of owning bonds is that there is a fixed rate that is paid over a set period of time. The disadvantage, depending on the type of bond invested in, is that a bond can default or lose value as the prevailing interest rate goes up or down.

Stocks – a stock, by definition, is a share or portion of ownership in a company that one is willing to purchase to become a shareholder of a particular company. By acquiring shares, the investor hopes the share value will increase based on the performance and growth of the company. The advantage is that as shares grow, the investor's investment grows.

The disadvantage is that if the company does not perform, the investor's value will decline. Further, if the company fails, the investor loses his/her money.

Mutual funds – mutual funds can be comprised of stocks, bonds, or a combination of both. A mutual fund is a portfolio that allows you to own many stocks or bonds within an individual vehicle. By definition, it is an investment vehicle made up of a pool of money from many investors for the purpose of investing in different types of investments. Some mutual funds are "managed funds" and some are "non-managed" or no-load funds. Each fund will have specific investment objectives. For example, a bond fund will invest in bonds and stay within the boundaries stated in the prospectus. A growth fund will (based on the objective) only invest primarily in growth companies. The spectrum can be from small cap stocks to large cap stocks and/or from domestic to international.

The advantage of investing into a mutual fund is you may be able to own shares in many different companies, and reduce your risk because of the number of companies in the funds and the professional management of your investments. A mutual fund, as a general rule, is an inexpensive way to have your investment managed and monitored. In addition, they can give you the diversification that is important to have.

The disadvantage can be the overall cost of the particular fund. If you are a do-it-yourselfer and have the ability and knowledge, you may be able to generate the same return with less cost using ETF funds. In addition, if taxes are an issue, the timing of a sale by a fund manager can have an adverse impact on your tax liability.

Annuities – most people have a fear when mentioning annuities. Annuities have been around since the Roman Empire. As a form of annual payment, annuities have been used as pensions for long periods of a person's life. Obviously, over time annuities have changed greatly. By definition, an annuity is an investment vehicle that is designed to accept funding and grow until the individual is ready to begin taken money out of it. It is the only investment that can insure an income for life.

Today there are many types of annuities. There are immediate annuities, fixed annuities, and variable annuities, just to name a few.

- An "immediate" annuity allows one to invest a certain amount of money and begin receiving a payout (income), possibly for life.
- A "fixed" annuity will specify a fixed percentage rate for a fixed period of time. The investor's principal and interest rate is guaranteed.
- A "variable" annuity is an annuity that allows an investor to invest in the market with certain guarantees. Today there are many types of variable annuities that can guarantee annual rates of return, lifetime payouts, and so on.

It is very important that when investing in annuities that you fully understand the product.

The disadvantage of annuities can be the restrictions on taking money out, and for variable annuities, the fees may become excessive. Again, know the details of any investment you make.

Life Insurance – investing in life insurance is also an option that can be used for life protection, and also as a "tax free" income stream. Because of the complexity of this type of investment, professional advice should be used. However, it is an alternative for those investors that have the discretionary income to spend on this type of investment.

CHAPTER 8

Financial Advisors

"The Simplification of Becoming a Millionaire" is not about doing it yourself. While many of you may feel as if you can, or may want to, "do-it-yourself", facts show that for many reasons, it does not get done. Unfortunately you may end up, down the road, with much less money than you need or than you would have had if you had used an advisor.

I have been giving financial advice in one way or another since 1973–74. As a personal representative, when 401(k)s were relatively new to employees with the firm I worked for, I was asked by many what they should do. At that time and to this day, I thought the most important things for people to understand were how the stock market worked, the advantages and disadvantages, and how investing could enhance their financial life.

The definition of a financial advisor is one who provides financial advice and guidance. A financial advisor can provide many services which include "financial roadmaps" (planning), money management, tax advice, estate planning, and debt reduction strategies, just to mention a few services.

I think a good financial advisor is one of the most important partners that you can have. An advisor is a person that can determine how well you live your life from a financial point of view. As I have said, you are far better off to pass away with a lot of money than to grow old with no money.

A financial advisor's most important role is primarily to do financial planning. Financial planning is very important because there will be many financial changes in your life that will have an impact on you. Changes in one form or another will occur approximately every nine to fourteen months. These changes can be positive or negative. Regardless, each change can impact you financially, positively or negatively.

For example, if you win the lottery, which is positive, and if you did not know how to plan and manage the money properly, you could end up not only broke but in worse shape than before you won. An advisor can help you make positive decisions to ensure the lottery winnings will enhance your life.

On the other hand, if a member of your family became disabled, had a long-term illness (which is negative), and did not have the knowledge or wherewithal to manage the problem, this can become a financial hardship.

Financial planning is very important because it helps you to develop a non-emotional financial roadmap to develop strategies and plans for current and future situations. As I indicated earlier, you don't know what you don't know.

A good financial advisor can help you to compartmentalize, coordinate, and carry out strategies to help get you where you need to be. If you are going on a vacation, you want to sit down, plan a trip, and plan things that you want to do prior to the vacation, as opposed to "flying by the seat of your pants." This can cause you to end up anywhere. Like the vacation trip, without proper planning, you could end up somewhere you don't want to be.

I believe you will get much farther ahead financially by using a professional than by trying to do it yourself. Obviously if you are trained, understand the ins and outs of planning and investing, and want to take the time to do it all, then do so. However, I have always found that using a professional, even with all of your knowledge, can be in your best interest.

In looking for a financial advisor, you want someone who has knowledge, experience, and who takes a personal interest in your financial life. First, have an idea of what you are looking for. For example, do you need someone that specializes in comprehensive planning? Or someone that specializes in education, healthcare, life insurance, or retirement? I recommend a "comprehensive" advisor. Just as important, know what they do.

In selecting an advisor, interview several (at least three) prospective advisors. Some advisors are "fee only" while others are "fee-based ." The difference between the two is that the "fee only" advisor one gets paid for giving advice only, while the "fee based" advisor gets paid for financial advice and products sold by the company they work for.

Two things here. One, don't be opposed to paying a fee to someone who will enhance your financial life. Two, don't be afraid to use an advisor that gives advice and sell products that their company sells. It bothers me to have someone say, "don't use an advisor that gives advice and sells products as well." I chose to work for a firm that allowed me to charge a fee for financial advice and to sell a whole spectrum of products that was appropriate for the clients.

I think it is a disservice to develop a financial plan for client and then tell them to go find someone else to implement the plan. It was very important to me, as an advisor, not only to provide the advice, but to give the client the opportunity to implement a plan with me. This way, I could properly manage their assets and ensure that their families were protected.

Once an advisor is selected and a plan and strategy are decided, you should meet with him/her on an ongoing basis. Based on the level of assets or complexity of your financial life, you may want to meet quarterly and no less than twice a year. Remember, your engagement in your financial life will dictate your success.

Lastly, don't get caught up in "high performance" investments. The most important thing is to get where you need to be when you need to be there. Early on in my career, I was given referrals on two occasions whereby when I met the prospects, one asked what rate of return he could expect. I told him, based on his needs, time frame, and asset allocation, he could expect a certain percent. He then told me that if I could not get him 45 to 50 percent return, there would be no reason to further meet with him. I thanked him for his time and gave him some "free advice." The advice was, "you need to be more diversified and realistic on your expected returns."

The second prospect had done well based on the performance of his 401(k) and the company stock that was in it. The prospect was within five years of retiring. After meeting with him he stated that he had done well by himself and the company would take care of him. I thanked him for his time and gave him some "free advice" as well. I informed him that he had done well because of the performance of the stock in his portfolio. However, since it was in company stock only and, in my opinion, the company was not that stable, he should consider more diversification. He laughed and said he would take his chances. Within a year, the stock had gone from almost $80 per share to about $.79 per share. The portfolio of almost $1,000,000 had declined to little over $80,000.

The point being, chasing returns will cause you to make poor, short-term decisions and not be properly diversified through asset allocation. In the two examples above, both individuals ended up losing a majority of their assets at a time and age that made it hard for them to recover. More than likely, they will be working a lot longer than they should have.

The use of a good advisor, in either of these cases, would have more than likely prevented their losses.

The purpose of this chapter is to encourage you to use an advisor as opposed to trying to do it yourself. A good advisor will want to know your goals, your thoughts and concerns, and work with you as a partner to help you become a millionaire.

Conclusion

"The Simplification of Becoming a Millionaire" is as simple as being committed to yourself and those that you care about. If you are willing to take the time and commit to knowing where you are and where you want to go financially, commit to finding and working with a good financial advisor, commit to "paying yourself" a portion of what you work hard for, and to commit to the discipline of these things, you can simply become a millionaire.

I cannot overemphasize the importance of money, time, and family. Some may disagree with the order. However, I think it is important to build your financial life first. While money isn't everything, it allows you to give you and your family the wherewithal to do the things you want to do. It allows you to afford the health care to live longer, and to remove the stress of being poor. As I've heard, you can be poor and have issues or you can be wealthy and have issues. Choose being wealthy with issues every time.

Time gives you the option to do a lot of things. It allows you to reset your decisions and your life. Almost everyone along the way will make mistakes, but the importance of making mistakes is to learn lessons from them. Along with the knowledge learned from mistakes and life experiences, they help make you smarter and wiser.

Take the time to make decisions that will enhance your life. Time is a precious commodity that is irreplaceable and once gone, cannot be gotten back. You should make every day a "reset" day. By this I mean, don't worry about what happened yesterday or what may happen tomorrow, but when you wake up today hit "reset", clearing the slate, and make today the type of day you want it to be.

Finally, the selection of your family partner (team member) is one of the most important decisions that you will make. Is this person someone that is bringing something to the table other than beauty and/or sex? They should be someone that knows your goals, understands your goals, and is willing to help you achieve your goals. It is important that your life partner and financial partner is committed to the same financial goals that you are.

It is important to keep everything in balance, whether it is work and play or save and spend. Every day should be lived as if it is your last. Try to use every second wisely. Things that you can do something about, do it. If it's something that you can't do anything about, forget about it and move forward.

Lastly, "The Simplification of Becoming a Millionaire" is simple. Like life, the simpler you make it, the more enjoyable it is. Your financial life should be simple. Know where you want to go financially, hire a professional, and enjoy the ride.

The time is now, and waiting means never doing it. So get set, go, and enjoy it all.

Epilogue

I have written this book as a way to pass on my knowledge to help the average person to realize that becoming a millionaire is not an unattainable goal, but one that can be achieved through simple steps. Using the approach I have talked about has helped many of my clients, who started with very little, become millionaires.

My journey, from a small, shoeless little boy, who, through hard work, saving and systematic investing, with a terrific life partner, not only changed my life, but gave me the opportunity to change others' lives as well.

I hope reading this book will help you to realize how "simple" it is to accumulate wealth and have an enjoyable life.

About the Author

Gary Clark was born in Summerfield North Carolina, served in the U.S. Navy, graduated from Guilford College, and is married to Linda. They have two children Tracy and Lee with four grandchildren Kyndall, Dylan, Alexander, and Ada. He is a retired financial advisor.

www.ingramcontent.com/pod-product-compliance
Lightning Source LLC
Chambersburg PA
CBHW021047180526
45163CB00005B/2325